FREELANCING

1. Introduction to Freelancing
   - What is freelancing?
   - Pros and Cons of Freelancing.
   - Why should you choose freelancing?
   - Different Freelancing Platforms.
   - Microservices or proposal-based freelancing.
2. Finding Your Niche
   - Identifying your skills and expertise
   - Researching the market demand for your skills
3. Setting Up Accounts
   - Create Accounts on different platforms.
   - Setting up your Profile.
4. Finding and Landing Clients
   - Searching for jobs
   - Pitching your services effectively

- Writing a high-quality proposal

- Writing a winning freelancing microservice

   - Closing the deal and negotiating rates
   - Communicating with clients.
   - Dealing with difficult clients
5. Managing Your Finances
   - Setting rates and pricing your services
   - Managing invoices and payments
   - Tracking your expenses and filing taxes

6. Building Your Brand
   - Creating a personal brand that aligns with your niche
   - Developing a strong online presence
   - Creating a marketing strategy to promote your services
7. Managing Your Time and Productivity
   - Setting up a schedule and sticking to it
   - Delegating tasks and outsourcing
   - Avoiding burnout and staying motivated
8. Expanding Your Freelance Business
   - Scaling your business through subcontracting or hiring employees
   - Creating passive income streams
   - Planning for the future of your freelance career
9. Dealing with Challenges
   - Handling difficult clients
   - Managing project scope and deadlines
   - Coping with periods of low income
10. Conclusion and Next Steps
    - Reflecting on your freelance journey
    - Setting goals for the future
    - Next steps for growing and improving your freelance business.
11. References

About the author:

As an author of this book, I bring with me a wealth of experience and expertise in the world of freelancing. I am proud to hold the title of Top-rated Freelancer on Upwork, as well as being a Level 5 Freelancer on PeoplePerHour.com. With 8 positive reviews on Freelancer.com, I have established a strong reputation in the industry. Additionally, I have taken on the role of a Freelancing Guru on Udacity, where I have had the privilege of training over 2000 students to become successful freelancers. Alongside my work as an author, I also contribute my skills as a remote Data Analyst for a US-based company. Through my diverse experiences, I am passionate about sharing valuable insights and knowledge to empower others in their freelance journeys.

INTRODUCTION TO FREELANCING

What is freelancing?

Freelancing is a type of work arrangement where a person, often called a freelancer or independent contractor, provides services to clients on a project-by-project or contractual basis rather than being employed full-time by a single company. In this arrangement, the freelancer is self-employed and has the freedom to choose their clients, set their own rates, and work on their own terms.

Freelancing can encompass a wide range of industries and services, including writing, graphic design, programming, consulting, marketing, and more. Freelancers can work from anywhere, if they have the necessary equipment and internet connection to complete their work.

One of the biggest advantages of freelancing is flexibility. Freelancers have the ability to choose when and where they work, allowing for a better work-life balance. They can also choose which clients and projects they take on, allowing them to focus on work that aligns with their skills and interests.

Another advantage of freelancing is the potential for higher earnings. Since freelancers set their own rates and can take on multiple clients simultaneously, they have the ability to earn more than they might in a traditional employment situation. However, it is important to note that freelancing can also be less stable and predictable than traditional employment, as work can be more sporadic, and income can vary from month to month.

In addition to the benefits, there are also some challenges associated with freelancing. Freelancers are responsible for finding their own clients and managing their own finances, which can be time-consuming and stressful. They also may not have access to benefits such as health insurance or retirement plans that are typically provided by employers.

Overall, freelancing can be a rewarding and lucrative career path for those with the skills and motivation to succeed in this type of

AHMED ATA

work arrangement.

Pros and Cons of Freelancing:

There are many advantages to freelancing. Here are some of the key benefits:

1. Flexibility: One of the biggest advantages of freelancing is the flexibility it offers. Freelancers can often choose their own work hours and work from anywhere with an internet connection, which can be a major advantage for those looking for a better work-life balance or those with other commitments, such as childcare or caring for a loved one.
2. Autonomy: Freelancers are their own bosses, which means they have greater control over their work and their career. They can choose which clients and projects they work on, and they have more say in how they approach their work.
3. Earning potential: Freelancers have the ability to set their own rates and take on multiple clients, which means they have the potential to earn more than they might in a traditional employment situation.
4. Variety: Freelancers have the opportunity to work on a variety of projects and with a variety of clients, which can keep their work interesting and engaging.
5. Skill development: Working on different projects with different clients can help freelancers develop a wider range of skills and knowledge, which can be valuable for their career growth.
6. No Commute: With no commute, freelancers can save time and money, and also reduce their carbon footprint.
7. Lower Overhead: Freelancers don't have the overhead of running an office or a traditional business, which can result in lower expenses and higher profits.

8. Independence: Freelancing provides a sense of independence and control over one's career that can be empowering and fulfilling.

Of course, there are also some challenges associated with freelancing, such as finding clients, managing finances, and dealing with an unpredictable workload. However, for those with the skills, motivation, and determination to succeed in this type of work arrangement, the advantages of freelancing can make it a very attractive career path.

While there are many benefits to freelancing, there are also some potential disadvantages to consider. Here are some of the most common challenges that freelancers may face:

1. Irregular Income: Freelancers don't have a guaranteed monthly salary and may face uneven cash flows as they complete projects and wait for payments. This can make it difficult to budget and plan for expenses, and can lead to financial stress during slow periods.

2. No Benefits: Freelancers are responsible for their own benefits, such as health insurance, paid time off, and retirement savings. This can add up to significant costs, and may mean that freelancers go without certain types of coverage or benefits.

3. No Job Security: Freelancers typically do not have long-term contracts with clients, and may not have guaranteed work from one project to the next. This lack of job security can be stressful, especially during slow periods or economic downturns.

4. Self-Employment Taxes: Freelancers are responsible for paying their own taxes, which can be complex and time-consuming. They may need to set aside a portion of their income to cover taxes, and may need to work with an accountant or tax professional to ensure they are complying with all relevant regulations.

5. Isolation: Freelancers often work from home or other remote locations, which can be isolating and lonely. They may miss the social interactions and professional development opportunities that come with working in an office or traditional employment setting.

6. Administrative Tasks: Freelancers are responsible for all aspects of their business, from marketing and sales to invoicing and project management. This can be time-consuming and take away from time that could be spent on billable work.

7. Difficult Clients: Freelancers may encounter difficult or demanding clients, who may be slow to pay, unreasonable in their requests, or difficult to work with. Freelancers need to be skilled in managing client relationships and setting boundaries in order to ensure successful projects.

While these disadvantages should not necessarily discourage individuals from pursuing a freelance career, it is important to be aware of the potential challenges and take steps to mitigate them. This might include developing a financial plan, setting up a support network of other freelancers, and learning how to manage difficult clients effectively.

Why should you choose freelancing?

Deciding whether freelancing is the right career path for you requires careful consideration of your personal and professional goals, as well as an honest assessment of your skills and temperament. Here are some signs that freelancing may be a good fit for you:

1. You value flexibility: If you value the ability to set your own schedule, work from anywhere, and take time off as needed, freelancing may be a good fit. Freelancing can provide greater control over your work-life balance, allowing you to prioritize your personal life and commitments.

2. You are self-motivated: Freelancing requires a high degree of self-motivation and discipline. You will need to be able to manage your own time, set and meet deadlines, and stay focused on your work without the structure of a traditional office environment.

3. You have a marketable skill set: Freelancing requires a marketable skill set that is in demand, such as writing, design, programming, or marketing. You will need to be able to demonstrate your expertise and provide value to clients in order to build a successful freelance career.

4. You enjoy working independently: Freelancing can be a solitary pursuit, requiring long hours of focused work without the social interactions of an office environment. If you enjoy working independently and are comfortable with solitude, freelancing may be a good fit.

5. You are comfortable with risk: Freelancing can be unpredictable, with uneven income, difficult clients, and a lack of job security. If you are comfortable with risk and are able to weather periods of uncertainty, freelancing may be a good fit.

Ultimately, deciding whether freelancing is right for you requires careful consideration of your personal and professional goals, as well as an honest assessment of your skills, temperament, and ability to manage the challenges of freelancing. If you are willing to put in the work and are comfortable with the risks and rewards of freelancing, it can be a rewarding and fulfilling career path.

Different Freelancing Platforms:

There are many freelancing platforms available, each with its own unique features and target audience. Here are some of the most popular freelancing platforms:

1. Upwork: Upwork is one of the largest freelancing platforms, with millions of registered freelancers and clients. It offers a wide range of job categories, including web development, design, writing, marketing, and more.
2. Freelancer: Freelancer is another popular freelancing platform, with a focus on web development, design, and IT-related projects. It offers a variety of project types, including fixed-price, hourly, and contests.
3. Fiverr: Fiverr is a popular platform for microservices, with many freelancers offering small, fixed-price services such as logo design, social media posts, and website optimization.
4. Toptal: Toptal is a platform for elite freelancers, with a rigorous vetting process that ensures a high level of quality and expertise. It specializes in software development, design, and finance.
5. PeoplePerHour: PeoplePerHour is a UK-based platform that offers a variety of job categories, including web development, design, writing, and marketing. It allows clients to post jobs or search for freelancers based on specific skills.
6. Guru: Guru is a platform that offers a variety of job categories, including web development, design, writing, marketing, and more. It offers a variety of payment options, including fixed-price, hourly, and recurring payments.
7. 99designs: 99designs is a platform that specializes in

graphic design, offering a variety of project types such as logos, websites, and packaging design. It uses a contest-based model, where clients choose from a variety of design submissions.

These are just a few of the many freelancing platforms available. When choosing a platform, it is important to consider factors such as the types of projects offered, the platform's fees and payment options, and the quality and quantity of freelancers available.

Microservices or proposal-based freelancing

Microservices and proposal-based freelancing are two different models of freelancing that offer different benefits and drawbacks.

Microservices freelancing involves offering small, pre-defined services at a fixed price. On platforms like Fiverr and Task Rabbit, freelancers offer specific services such as designing a logo or writing a short article, and clients can purchase those services directly. Microservices freelancing is generally a more transactional approach, with less emphasis on building long-term relationships with clients.

Proposal-based freelancing, on the other hand, involves submitting proposals for larger, more complex projects. On platforms like Upwork and Freelancer, clients post job listings and freelancers submit proposals outlining their qualifications and how they would approach the project. Proposal-based freelancing is generally a more collaborative approach, with a greater emphasis on building long-term relationships with clients.

There are benefits and drawbacks to each approach. Microservices freelancing can be a good way to generate quick income and build a portfolio of work. However, it can be difficult to make a sustainable income solely through microservices, as there is a limit to how many services a freelancer can realistically offer at a given price point.

Proposal-based freelancing can be a good way to build relationships with clients and work on larger, more complex projects. However, it can be time-consuming to submit proposals and compete with other freelancers, and there is no guarantee that a proposal will be accepted or result in ongoing work.

Ultimately, the right approach to freelancing depends on the freelancer's skills, goals, and target market. Some freelancers may find success with a mix of both approaches, offering microservices to generate quick income and submitting proposals for larger projects to build relationships with clients.

FINDING YOUR NICHE

Identifying your skills and expertise

Identifying your skills and expertise is an important step in starting a successful freelancing career. As a freelancer, you will need to market yourself and your skills to potential clients, so it is important to have a clear understanding of what you can offer and what sets you apart from other freelancers.

Here are some steps to help you identify your skills and expertise:

1. Evaluate your work experience: Take a close look at your past work experience, including any jobs, internships, or volunteer work you have done. What skills did you develop in these roles? What did you enjoy doing? What types of tasks or projects were you particularly good at?

2. Consider your education and training: Think about any degrees, certifications, or training programs you have completed. What skills did you gain from these programs? Are there any areas where you have specialized knowledge or expertise?

3. Reflect on your hobbies and interests: What are you passionate about outside of work? Do you have any hobbies or interests that could translate into a marketable skill? For example, if you enjoy photography, you could offer your services as a freelance photographer.

4. Look at current job trends: Research current job trends in your industry or field. Are there any emerging skills or areas of expertise that are in high demand? Could you develop these skills and market yourself as an expert in these areas?

5. Ask for feedback: Talk to friends, family members, or former colleagues to get their perspective on your skills and strengths. They may be able to offer insights that you hadn't considered.

Once you have identified your skills and expertise, you can begin to build a portfolio that showcases your work and highlights your strengths. This could include examples of your past work, testimonials from clients or colleagues, and descriptions of your skills and expertise.

The top paid jobs in freelancing can vary depending on the industry, location, and demand for specific skills. However, here are some freelancing jobs that are generally considered high-paying:

1. Web Development: Web development is a highly in-demand field, with many businesses looking to build or update their websites. Skilled web developers can command high rates for their services, particularly if they specialize in popular frameworks and languages such as React, Angular, or Node.js.
2. Mobile Development: Mobile app development is another in-demand field, as many businesses seek to create mobile apps for their customers. Experienced mobile developers can earn high hourly rates for their work.
3. Data Science and Analytics: With the growing importance of data in business decision-making, there is a high demand for data scientists and analysts. These professionals can earn high hourly rates for their ability to analyze and interpret complex data sets.
4. Graphic Design: Graphic designers are needed to create logos, marketing materials, and other visual assets for businesses. Skilled designers with a strong portfolio can command high hourly rates.
5. Copywriting: Copywriters are skilled at writing compelling content that engages audiences and drives sales. Experienced copywriters can earn high hourly rates for their work, particularly if they specialize in a specific industry or niche.

6. Digital Marketing: Digital marketing is a broad field that includes search engine optimization (SEO), pay-per-click (PPC) advertising, social media marketing, and more. Skilled digital marketers can earn high hourly rates for their ability to drive traffic and conversions for businesses.

7. Video Production: Video is becoming an increasingly important medium for businesses, with many seeking to create promotional videos, explainer videos, and other types of video content. Experienced video producers can command high hourly rates for their work.

8. Project Management: Project managers are responsible for overseeing the planning, execution, and delivery of projects. Skilled project managers with experience in a specific industry or niche can earn high hourly rates for their ability to deliver projects on time and within budget.

It is worth noting that the rates for these freelance jobs can vary widely depending on location, experience, and industry. However, with the right skills and experience, freelancers in these fields can command high hourly rates and build successful, high-paying careers.

Remember, as a freelancer, you will need to be flexible and adaptable. You may need to adjust your skills and expertise to meet the needs of different clients or industries. But by starting with a clear understanding of your strengths and what you can offer, you will be better positioned to find success as a freelancer.

Researching the market demand for your skills

Researching the market demand for your skills is a critical step in starting a successful freelancing career. By understanding the demand for your skills, you can better position yourself in the market, set competitive rates, and identify potential clients.

Here are some steps to help you research the market demand for your skills:

1. Look at job boards and freelancing platforms: Check out job boards such as Indeed, Glassdoor, or LinkedIn, as well as freelancing platforms like Upwork or Freelancer. Search for jobs or projects that require your skills and take note of how many job postings there are, what the average rates are, and what type of companies are posting these jobs.

2. Analyze industry trends: Keep up with industry news and trends to understand what skills are in demand. This could include reading industry blogs or news articles, attending industry conferences or webinars, or following influencers on social media.

3. Use online tools: There are several online tools available that can help you research market demand for your skills. For example, Google Trends can help you identify the search volume for specific keywords related to your skills, while LinkedIn's Workforce Report can provide insights into industry trends and job demand.

4. Talk to potential clients: Reach out to potential clients or industry contacts to get a sense of what types of skills are in demand. You could do this through informational interviews or by attending networking events.

5. Identify your competition: Research other freelancers or businesses that offer similar services to yours. Look at their rates, portfolio, and marketing strategies to

understand how you can differentiate yourself from the competition.

By understanding the demand for your skills, you can better position yourself in the market and target clients that are most likely to need your services. This can help you set competitive rates and build a successful freelancing career. Keep in mind that demand for specific skills can change over time, so it is important to stay up-to-date on industry trends and adapt your skills and services as needed.

SETTING UP YOUR ACCOUNTS

Creating a profile

Creating a profile on freelancing platforms is an important step in establishing your presence as a freelancer and attracting potential clients. Here's a more detailed explanation of what should be included in your profile:

1. Name and photo: Use your real name and a professional photo to build credibility and trust with potential clients. A clear, high-quality headshot is recommended.

2. Professional headline: Your professional headline should be a brief, attention-grabbing statement that describes your area of expertise and the services you offer. It should be focused on what you can do for clients and should highlight your unique selling proposition.

3. Summary: In your profile, include a brief summary of your skills and experience. This should include the industries you have worked in, the type of work you specialize in, and any specific skills or tools you use. Be sure to highlight your strengths and any unique skills or experience that set you apart from other freelancers.

4. Portfolio: Your portfolio should showcase your best work and demonstrate your skills and experience. Include examples of previous work you have completed that are relevant to the types of projects you are seeking. This can be in the form of links to websites or online content, images or videos, or PDFs of previous work.

5. Rates and availability: You may choose to include your rates and availability in your profile, although this is not always necessary. If you do include your rates, be sure to set them at a competitive level based on your skills and experience.

6. Top Skills: In the top skills part you should mention all the skills you have, and you are experienced in. These skills will make your profile appear in the clients search

results. And it can increase your Bid ranking when it matches any project requirements.

7. Experience and Education: In this part you can mention any previous Experience you have even if not related to the headline, and you can mention the Education you have.
8. Qualifications: In this part you can mention the main Courses and Nano degrees you have with some details about each one.
9. Many platforms allow you to take skill exams that will increase your chances to land Gigs. As skill exams on freelancing platforms are a valuable tool for both freelancers and clients, as they can help to provide an objective assessment of a freelancer's abilities and level of expertise in a particular area.
10. Completing the Identity Verification, also known as Know Your Customer (KYC).

Setting up your profile

Your profile is often the first impression that potential clients will have of you, so it is important to make it as professional and polished as possible. Be sure to proofread your profile for errors and typos and use a clear and concise writing style. Including a professional-looking headshot and a portfolio of your best work can help to establish your credibility and attract more clients. As you gain more experience and receive positive feedback from clients, be sure to update your profile to reflect your growth and accomplishments.

1. Name And Photo

When creating a freelancer profile, the name and photo are important components that can affect how potential clients perceive you. Here are some best practices for choosing a name and photo for your freelancer profile:

1. Use your real name: It's important to use your real name rather than a nickname or pseudonym. This builds credibility and trust with potential clients.
2. Choose a professional photo: Your profile photo should be a clear, high-quality headshot that presents you as a professional. Avoid using selfies or photos with distracting backgrounds.
3. Dress professionally: Dress in a way that is appropriate for your industry and the type of work you do. If you work in a creative field, you may be able to get away with a more casual look, but if you work in a more formal industry, you should dress accordingly.
4. Use a consistent photo across all platforms: If you have profiles on multiple freelancing platforms, use the same photo on all of them. This makes it easier for potential clients to recognize you and helps to establish your

personal brand.

5. Avoid using stock photos: Using stock photos or generic images can make your profile seem less authentic and may turn off potential clients.

6. Smile: A friendly, approachable smile can help to build rapport with potential clients and make them more likely to want to work with you.

Overall, your name and photo should present you as a professional and convey your personality and style. They should be consistent across all of your online profiles and should help to build trust and credibility with potential clients.

2. Professional Headline

A professional headline is an important part of a freelancer's profile. It is the first thing that potential clients see when they visit your profile and it should give them a clear idea of your skills and expertise. Here are some best practices for creating a professional headline for your freelancer profile:

1. Be clear and concise: Your professional headline should be clear and concise, ideally no more than 10 words. It should convey what you do and the services you offer in a straightforward way.

2. Use keywords: Incorporate keywords into your headline

that are relevant to your industry and the type of work you do. This will help potential clients find you when they search for freelancers with specific skills or experience.

3. Highlight your unique selling proposition: Your professional headline should highlight what sets you apart from other freelancers. This might include your specific expertise, your level of experience, or any specialized skills or tools you use.

4. Tailor your headline to your audience: Your professional headline should be tailored to the audience you are targeting. If you are targeting clients in a specific industry, for example, you may want to include industry-specific keywords in your headline.

5. Avoid using buzzwords or jargon: While it's important to use keywords in your headline, you should avoid using buzzwords or jargon that may not be familiar to potential clients.

Here are some examples of how to write a headline for different positions:

- Content writer: Experienced Content Writer with a focus on SEO and social media marketing.
- Graphic designer: Creative Graphic Designer with a passion for branding and visual storytelling.
- Web developer: Full-Stack Web Developer specializing in JavaScript and React.
- Social media manager: Social Media Manager with a track record of driving engagement and increasing brand awareness.
- Virtual assistant: Skilled Virtual Assistant with expertise in administrative support and project management.

In case you want to add more than one specialization they

should be related as
- Data Analyst | Data Scientist | Python Developer

Data Analysis | Data Science | Python Programming

In each of these examples, the headline clearly conveys what the freelancer does and what their specific skills and expertise are. They use keywords and highlight the freelancer's unique selling proposition, while avoiding buzzwords or jargon. By following these best practices, you can create a professional headline that helps to attract potential clients and establish your personal brand.

◆ ◆ ◆

3. Summary or About section

The "About" or "Summary" section of your freelancer profile is an important opportunity to introduce yourself and your services to potential clients. Here are some best practices to follow when crafting this section:

1. Keep it concise: Your summary should be brief and to the point, highlighting your key skills and experience in a clear and concise manner.
2. Use keywords: Including relevant keywords can help your profile show up in search results and make it easier for potential clients to find you.
3. Focus on the benefits you offer: Instead of just listing your skills and experience, focus on the benefits you can offer to clients. For example, instead of saying "I am a web designer," you could say "I create user-friendly

websites that help businesses increase conversions."

4. Highlight your unique value proposition: What sets you apart from other freelancers in your field? Do you have a unique skill set or approach? Be sure to highlight this in your summary.

5. Use a conversational tone: Your summary should be written in a conversational tone that feels approachable and friendly. Avoid using overly technical language or jargon.

6. Show some personality: Don't be afraid to inject a little bit of personality into your summary. This can help you stand out and make a connection with potential clients.

7. Mention some of the past projects you worked on.

8. Divide the summary into paragraphs for easier reading.

9. Add your best skills as bullet points.

By following these best practices, you can create an effective summary that showcases your skills and experience and helps you stand out to potential clients.

Ahmed is a Data Scientist with more than 3 years of coding experience, in the fields of Data Analysis, Data Visualization, Machine learning.

Professional in:
✅ Python, Pandas, Numpy for Data Analytics.
✅ Matplotlib, Seaborn for Visualization.
✅ Sklearn Machine Learning.
✅ PyTorch Deep Learning
✅ TensorFlow/Keras Deep Learning.
✅ Tableau Dashboards
✅ Analyzing OCR results from AWS Textract and Azure FormRecognizer

Ahmed has Worked on many projects as:

- Ford Go Bike share data Exploration.
- Analyze A/B Test results with Logistic Regression.
- WeRateDogs Twitter Page Data EDA.
- Kaggle 2020 survey data analysis competition.
- Building Flower Images Classifier using Tensorflow and Keras.
- Identify Customer Segments using KMeans and PCA.
- Face generation using GANs.
- Generating TV scripts using LSTMs using PyTorch.
- Machine Translation using RNNs.
- Twitter scraper Web application.

4. Portfolio

The portfolio section of your freelancer profile is an important opportunity to showcase your work and provide evidence of your skills and experience. Here are some best practices to follow when creating your portfolio:

1. Include your best work: Choose your best and most relevant work to include in your portfolio. Quality is more important than quantity, so only include your strongest pieces.

2. Provide context: For each piece in your portfolio, provide a brief description of the project and your role in it. This helps potential clients understand the context of your work and how it relates to their needs.

3. Organize your portfolio: Organize your portfolio in a way that makes sense and is easy to navigate. You might choose to group your work by project type, industry, or skill set.
4. Use visuals: Include high-quality visuals of your work, such as screenshots, videos, or images. This helps potential clients get a sense of your design aesthetic and the quality of your work.
5. Provide results: Whenever possible, include measurable results or statistics that demonstrate the impact of your work. This can help potential clients understand the value you can provide.
6. Keep it up to date: Regularly update your portfolio with new and relevant work as you complete projects. This helps to keep your profile fresh and up to date.
7. If you don't have many work samples yet, you can add some samples from the projects you made in courses. And you can also add screenshots of your certificates.
8. Make sure to ask for a client's permission if you want to add the work you did for him in your portfolio.

◆ ◆ ◆

5. Rates And Availability

Setting your rates and availability in your freelancer profile is an important part of attracting clients and managing your workload. Here are some best practices to follow when setting your rates and availability:

1. Research industry standards: Research industry standards and rates for your particular skillset and experience level. This will help you set rates that are competitive and realistic.
2. Be transparent: Be transparent about your rates and availability in your profile. Clients appreciate transparency and honesty, and it helps to manage their expectations from the outset.
3. Consider your experience level: If you are just starting out, you may want to consider setting lower rates initially to attract clients and build your portfolio. As you gain experience and reputation, you can gradually raise your rates.
4. Offer package deals: Consider offering package deals or bundled services to encourage clients to choose you over competitors.
5. Be flexible: Be open to negotiating rates and terms with clients, particularly if the project scope changes or if the client has a limited budget.
6. Update regularly: Regularly update your rates and availability to reflect changes in your schedule or experience level.

By following these best practices, you can set rates and availability that are competitive, transparent, and flexible, which will help you attract and retain clients over time.

Some Platforms are very competitive, and you may need to start with a low rate and increase it step by step (I started with 5$ and increased my rate 1$ after each successful Job).

6. Top Skills:

The skills section of your freelancer profile is an important part of showcasing your expertise and helping clients understand what you can offer. Here are some best practices to follow when selecting and highlighting your top skills:

1. Choose your strongest skills: Identify your strongest and most in-demand skills and highlight them in your profile. Focus on the skills that you are most experienced in and that are most relevant to the work you want to do.
2. Be specific: Use specific keywords and phrases that accurately describe your skills. This will help clients find you when searching for freelancers with particular skillsets.
3. Update regularly: Regularly update your skills section as your experience and expertise grows. This ensures that your profile remains up-to-date and accurately reflects your capabilities.
4. Most platforms will allow a limited number of skills to be added with the basic plan so make sure to add your most top skills. If you can add more skills make sure to add skills that may have different words and Analysis and Analytics.
5. These skills are import as Most platforms has an algorithm that ranks the proposals based on how many skills are matched with the job requirements.

7. Experience And Education:

When it comes to the experience and education sections of your freelancer profile, there are a few best practices to keep in mind to help you effectively showcase your professional background and qualifications:

1. Focus on relevant experience: Highlight your most relevant work experience, focusing on projects that are most similar to the type of work you want to do as a freelancer. Be sure to include details about your role and responsibilities, as well as any notable achievements or outcomes.
2. Use specific metrics: Whenever possible, use specific metrics to demonstrate the impact of your work. For example, if you worked on a project that resulted in increased website traffic, include the percentage increase you achieved.
3. Highlight transferable skills: Even if you don't have extensive experience in a particular industry or skillset, highlight transferable skills that are relevant to the work you want to do as a freelancer. For example, if you have project management experience, highlight your ability to manage timelines and budgets.
4. Add at the end any experiences you have that may not be relative to your headline.
5. Be concise: Keep your descriptions of your experience and education brief and to the point. Avoid jargon and technical terms that may not be familiar to all clients.
6. Show education and certifications: Include information about your education and any relevant certifications or training. This can help demonstrate your expertise and qualifications.

7. Provide links: Provide links to your portfolio, LinkedIn profile, or other relevant websites or resources where clients can learn more about your experience and qualifications.

8. Qualifications:

In this part you can add more details about the different Courses you have. Mentioning the main subjects of each course and what you have learned.

9. Skill Exams:

Here are some of the key benefits of taking skill exams on freelancing platforms:

1. Demonstrate expertise: Skill exams can help to demonstrate a freelancer's expertise in a particular area, providing clients with confidence that they have the necessary skills to complete a project.

2. Stand out from the competition: By taking and passing skill exams, freelancers can differentiate themselves from other freelancers on the platform who may not have taken the exams or who may not have performed as well.

3. Increase visibility: Some freelancing platforms may

feature freelancers who have taken and performed well on skill exams, increasing their visibility to potential clients.

4. Improve credibility: Skill exams can help to improve a freelancer's credibility and reputation on the platform, as clients can see objective evidence of their skills and expertise.

5. Expand opportunities: Freelancers who perform well on skill exams may be invited to apply for additional projects or receive preferential treatment from clients.

Overall, taking skill exams can be a valuable investment for freelancers looking to build their reputation and increase their opportunities for work on freelancing platforms. By demonstrating their expertise and standing out from the competition, freelancers can increase their chances of being hired for high-quality projects and building long-term relationships with clients

10. Identity Verification:

Completing The Identity Verification, Also Known As Know Your Customer (Kyc), On Freelancing Platforms Is An Important Step For Both Freelancers And Clients. Kyc Is A Process Of Verifying The Identity Of A User, Which Typically Involves Submitting Personal Information And Government-Issued Identification To The Platform.

Here Are Some Reasons Why Completing The Kyc Process Is

Important:

    a. Trust and safety: By completing the KYC process, freelancers can establish trust with clients and demonstrate that they are a legitimate and trustworthy professional. Clients are often more likely to hire freelancers who have completed the KYC process because it helps to reduce the risk of fraud and scams.

    b. Access to premium features: Some freelancing platforms may offer premium features that are only available to users who have completed the KYC process. These features may include access to higher-paying projects, increased visibility on the platform, and priority support.

    c. Compliance with regulations: Freelancing platforms are required to comply with various regulations related to money laundering and fraud prevention. By completing the KYC process, freelancers can help ensure that the platform remains compliant with these regulations.

    d. Avoiding account suspension: Failure to complete the KYC process may result in the suspension or termination of a freelancer's account on the platform. This can result in the loss of ongoing projects, reviews, and ratings.

Overall, completing the KYC process is an important step in establishing trust and credibility on freelancing platforms. Freelancers who complete the process are more likely to attract high-quality clients and access premium features, while also ensuring compliance with regulatory requirements and avoiding the risk of account suspension.

AHMED ATA

FINDING AND LANDING CLIENTS

A client refers to an individual, organization, or business entity that hires and engages the services of a freelancer to fulfill a specific project or task. The client is the party that seeks the expertise, skills, and deliverables provided by the freelancer. They are typically the ones who initiate the project, define the requirements, and set the expectations for the desired outcome.

Clients in the freelancing world play a crucial role in determining the scope of work, timelines, and budget for a project. They may have a specific goal or objective in mind and rely on the freelancer's expertise to achieve it. Clients can be individuals, small businesses, startups, or large corporations across various industries.

Clients may approach freelancers directly, through freelancing platforms, or through referrals. They seek freelancers with the necessary skills, experience, and qualifications to meet their project needs. It is the client's responsibility to provide clear project requirements, provide feedback and direction throughout the process, and ultimately evaluate the deliverables provided by the freelancer.

Successful freelancers prioritize effective communication, understanding client needs, and delivering high-quality work that aligns with the client's expectations. Building positive relationships with clients can lead to repeat business, referrals, and a solid reputation in the freelancing community.

Types Of The Clients:

As a freelancer, you can encounter various types of clients with different needs, preferences, and working styles. Here are some common types of clients that you may come across:

1. Individual Clients: These are individuals who require freelancers for their personal projects. They could be entrepreneurs, small business owners, bloggers, authors, or individuals seeking creative or technical assistance.
2. Small and Medium-Sized Enterprises (SMEs): SMEs often seek freelancers to fulfill specific tasks or projects within their organizations. They may have limited resources or prefer to outsource certain functions, such as graphic design, content writing, web development, or marketing.
3. Startups: Startups are newly established businesses with unique needs and fast-paced environments. Freelancers can provide specialized skills and expertise to help startups launch their products or services, develop their branding, or assist with specific tasks.
4. Agencies: Creative or digital marketing agencies may hire freelancers to support their projects or handle overflow work. These agencies act as intermediaries between freelancers and clients, providing a steady stream of projects and managing client relationships.
5. Corporations: Large corporations often have in-house teams, but they may also engage freelancers for specific projects or specialized skills that are not available within their organizations. Freelancers can provide a fresh perspective, specialized expertise, or assist with temporary work spikes.
6. Non-Profit Organizations: Non-profit organizations

may require freelancers to assist with fundraising campaigns, website development, content creation, event planning, or other specific projects. Working with non-profits can provide an opportunity to contribute to meaningful causes.

7. International Clients: With the advent of technology and remote work, freelancers have the opportunity to work with clients from around the world. International clients can bring diverse perspectives, unique projects, and potentially higher-paying opportunities.

8. Repeat Clients: Building strong relationships with clients can lead to repeat business. Clients who have had a positive experience working with you may come back for additional projects or recommend you to others. Repeat clients can provide a stable and consistent source of work.

9. Referral Clients: Referral clients are those who come to you based on recommendations from previous clients, colleagues, or your professional network. These clients often have a level of trust and confidence in your abilities, making the working relationship smoother.

10. Niche or Industry-Specific Clients: Depending on your expertise, you may attract clients within a specific niche or industry. These clients value your specialized knowledge and understanding of their industry-specific needs.

Searching for jobs

After setting the profile and completing the verifications. You will need to search for relevant jobs, and to get the most relevant and suitable jobs you will have to follow some guidelines.

Here are some best practices for searching for jobs on freelancing platforms:

1. Define your search criteria: Before searching for jobs, define your search criteria based on your skills, experience, and preferences. This can include factors such as project type, budget, duration, location, and more.
2. Use relevant keywords: Use relevant keywords in your search to narrow down the results to jobs that are most relevant to your skills and experience.
3. Sort by relevance: Most freelancing platforms offer the ability to sort search results by relevance, date, or other factors. Sorting by relevance can help you see the most relevant jobs first, based on your search criteria and skills.
4. Review the job description carefully: Once you find a job that you are interested in, review the job description carefully to ensure that it aligns with your skills and experience. Look for details such as project requirements, deliverables, and deadlines to determine if the job is a good fit for you.
5. Check the client's feedback and rating: Before applying for a job, check the client's feedback and rating on the platform. This can give you an idea of the client's reputation and history of working with freelancers.
6. You may need to target entry level jobs at first as some Platforms like Upwork classifies jobs based on the Experience level.

Some platforms as Freelancer.com contain a different type of Jobs called Contests, Contests on Freelancer.com are competitions in which clients post a project brief and invite freelancers to submit their entries to complete the project. Contests can be a good way for freelancers to showcase their skills and win new clients.

Here's how contests work on Freelancer.com:

1. A client posts a project brief and sets a prize amount.
2. Freelancers submit their entries, which can include designs, written content, or other deliverables.
3. The client reviews the entries and selects a winner.
4. The winner receives the prize amount and is awarded the project.

Contests can be a good option for clients who are looking for creative solutions to a problem or want to see a range of different approaches to a project. For freelancers, contests can be a way to demonstrate their skills and build their portfolio, even if they don't win the prize.

It's important to note that contests on Freelancer.com can be competitive, with many freelancers submitting entries for the same project. To increase your chances of winning a contest, it's important to carefully read the project brief, follow the guidelines, and submit high-quality work that meets the client's needs.

Contests are very good choice for new Freelancers especially those who are afraid of getting a first bad review as the entries doesn't depend on your previous Feedback or previous Ratings, and if you the client didn't buy your Entry you will not get a bad review.

Pitching your services effectively

Pitching your services effectively is a critical part of winning freelance work. It requires you to be strategic, focused, and compelling in the way you present yourself and your skills to potential clients.

Here are some key elements of an effective pitch:

1. Personalization: When you pitch your services, it's important to show that you understand the client's needs and are offering a solution that is tailored to their specific requirements. This means taking the time to read the job description carefully and customizing your pitch accordingly. Use the client's name in your introduction and reference specific details from the job description to demonstrate your understanding of the project.

2. Value proposition: Your pitch should clearly articulate the value you bring to the client's project. This means highlighting your strengths, showcasing your experience and expertise, and explaining how you can help the client achieve their goals. Use concrete examples and data to demonstrate the impact you've had in similar projects.

3. Relevance: Your pitch should be focused on the client's needs and requirements. Don't include irrelevant information or generic statements that could apply to any project. Instead, demonstrate how your skills and experience are directly relevant to the project at hand.

4. Clarity: Your pitch should be easy to understand and free of jargon or technical terms that the client may not be familiar with. Use clear, concise language and avoid complex sentence structures.

5. Professionalism: Your pitch should demonstrate your professionalism and attention to detail. Use correct

grammar, spelling, and punctuation, and ensure that your pitch is well-organized and easy to read. Include a polite and professional closing that invites the client to contact you to discuss the project further.

By following these best practices, you can create a pitch that effectively communicates your skills and expertise, demonstrates your value proposition, and convinces potential clients to hire you for their projects.

Writing A High-Quality Proposal

In case of searching for jobs you will need to send a high-quality proposal, as this is one of the most important steps in freelancing, because clients hate when freelancers just send a template proposal to any job, they want to know that you really can solve their problem, and this is your chance to prove how experience you are.

These are some guidelines to write a high-quality proposal:

1. Read the job description thoroughly.
    3. start with a 'Hi' and add the client's name if possible.
    4. Make sure your proposal is tailored to the job description and not just copy paste template.
    5. Make sure your grammar is correct so the client can see you are professional. (Use Grammarly extension on your browser)
    6. write your best skills that matches the job requirements.
    7. write about previous projects that are like the job.
    8. divide your proposal into paragraphs for easier reading.
    9. end with a closure as ' I am looking forward to working with you' or a Call to action as "I am waiting for your message to discuss all the possible solution to this project."

10. Show your enthusiasm: Let the client know that you are excited about the project and interested in working with them.
11. Address any concerns: If there are any concerns or potential roadblocks related to the project, address them upfront in your proposal.
12. Include relevant samples: If you have any relevant samples of your work that demonstrate your skills and expertise, be sure to include them in your proposal.
13. Offer suggestions: If you have any suggestions or ideas for how the project could be improved or optimized, share them with the client.
14. Provide a timeline: Let the client know how long you anticipate the project will take and when you can deliver the final product.
15. Be competitive with your pricing: Make sure that your pricing is competitive and in line with industry standards.
16. Follow up: If you don't hear back from the client within a few days, follow up with a friendly message to reiterate your interest in the project.

Overall, the key to a successful proposal is to demonstrate your skills and expertise, show your enthusiasm for the project, and provide the client with all the information they need to make an informed decision.

Writing A Winning Freelancing Microservice

In case of Microservices you will not have to search for jobs, but you need to make an appealing and winning offer.

Here are some tips to create a winning freelancing microservice:

1. Identify a specific need: Focus on a specific need or problem that your target clients have. This could be a specific skill or task that they struggle with.
2. Define the scope of the service: Clearly define what the client can expect from the service. This includes the specific tasks you will perform, the expected outcomes, and the timeline for completion.
3. Keep it simple and focused: Your microservices should be clear and easy to understand. Focus on the specific skills and services you offer and avoid overwhelming potential clients with too much information.
4. Showcase your expertise: Highlight your expertise and experience in the area. This could include your qualifications, past work examples, and testimonials from satisfied clients.
5. Provide clear pricing: Make sure your pricing is transparent and easy to understand. Consider offering different pricing packages that suit the needs of different clients.
6. Offer outstanding customer service: Be responsive, professional, and friendly when communicating with potential clients. This can help build trust and a positive relationship.
7. Use persuasive language: Use persuasive language to convince potential clients of the value of your service. This could include highlighting the benefits, showcasing your expertise, and using testimonials or case studies.
8. Optimize your microservice for search: Use relevant keywords in the title and description of your microservice to improve its visibility in search results.

Remember that a winning microservice is not just about the service itself, but also about the way you present it to potential clients. By focusing on the specific needs of your target clients, showcasing your expertise, and providing outstanding customer service, you can create a winning freelancing microservice that attracts high-quality clients.

Closing the deal and negotiating rates

Closing the deal and negotiating rates with the client is an important aspect of freelancing. It requires effective communication skills and a clear understanding of the value of your services. Here are some tips for closing the deal and negotiating rates:

1. Discuss the scope of the project: Before discussing rates, make sure you have a clear understanding of the scope of the project. Ask questions to clarify any doubts you may have. And make sure you have all the skills required for the job and you can complete before the deadline.

2. Determine your rate: Based on the scope of the project and your skills, determine a rate that is reasonable and reflects the value of your services. Remember you can change the rate you suggested in the proposal if the job requires more work than described in the job description.

3. Present your rate: When presenting your rate to the client, be confident and explain how it aligns with the value you bring to the project. Provide examples of similar projects you have worked on and the results you achieved.

4. Negotiate if necessary: If the client proposes a rate lower than your rate, be prepared to negotiate. Be open to compromise and consider other factors such as the scope of the project, the timeline, and the potential for future work.

5. Set clear terms: Once you have agreed on a rate, make sure to set clear terms for the project. This includes the scope of work, deadlines, milestones, payment terms, how you will communicate with the client and what should you deliver when the work is completed.

6. Be honest with the client about your skills, if you need to study some skill explain that to the client and he may allow you to do that.
7. Get it in writing: It's important to have a written agreement that outlines the terms of the project. This can help avoid any misunderstandings or disputes down the road.
8. Follow up: After closing the deal, follow up with the client regularly to ensure the project is on track and to address any concerns or issues that may arise.

Remember, effective communication is key to closing the deal and negotiating rates with clients. Be confident, professional, and transparent throughout the process, and you'll be more likely to secure the project and build a successful freelance career.

Communicating with the client

Communicating with the client is a crucial part of freelancing. Here are some main points to consider:

1. Be professional: Keep the tone of your communication professional, polite and respectful. Always use proper grammar and spelling, and avoid using slang or overly casual language.

2. Respond in a timely manner: Respond to the client's messages or emails as soon as possible, within 24 hours at the latest. This shows the client that you are reliable and interested in the project.

3. Be clear and concise: Make sure you understand the client's requirements and ask questions if necessary. Provide clear and concise information in your communication, and avoid using technical jargon that the client may not understand.

4. Set realistic expectations: Be realistic about what you can deliver and when you can deliver it. Don't overpromise and underdeliver. If you need more time or if there are any issues, communicate this to the client as soon as possible.

5. Update regularly: Keep the client informed of your progress and update them regularly on the status of the project. This helps build trust and ensures that the client knows what is happening.

6. Handle conflicts professionally: If there are any issues or conflicts with the client, handle them professionally and respectfully. Try to find a solution that works for both parties.

7. If the client needs more work than what you agreed to do, ask him to make a new milestone in case of fixed rate jobs, but In case of hourly rate there will be no problem. But make sure this will not conflict with other jobs you

may planned to do.

Dealing with difficult clients

Dealing with difficult clients can be a challenging experience for freelancers, but it is a crucial skill to master in order to maintain a successful freelancing career. Here are some tips on how to deal with difficult clients:

1. Keep calm and professional:

Keeping calm and professional is an important tip when dealing with difficult clients. This means staying level-headed and composed, even when faced with challenging or frustrating situations. It's essential to maintain a professional demeanor and communicate in a polite and respectful manner at all times.

When a client is difficult, it's natural to feel frustrated, defensive, or angry. However, it's important not to let these emotions take over and to remain calm and professional in all interactions. This can help to diffuse tense situations and prevent them from escalating further.

To keep calm and professional, it can be helpful to take a step back and assess the situation objectively. Try to separate your emotions from the situation and focus on finding a solution. Take a deep breath, pause before responding, and choose your words carefully.

It's also important to avoid getting defensive or taking things personally. Remember that the client's frustration or anger is not necessarily directed at you personally, but rather at the situation or issue at hand. Try to listen to their concerns and respond with empathy and understanding.

2. Be detail specific:

Being detail-specific can help in dealing with difficult clients by providing clarity and avoiding misunderstandings. When communicating with difficult clients, it's important to be as clear and specific as possible about what you can and cannot do, what the project entails, and what the client can expect from you.

For example, if a difficult client is requesting a change that you cannot accommodate, explain in detail why it is not possible and offer alternative solutions. Similarly, if a difficult client is not clear about their expectations or requirements, ask for more information and provide detailed explanations of how you can meet their needs.

By being detail-specific, you can demonstrate your expertise and professionalism, and help to build trust and confidence with the difficult client. It also allows you to set clear boundaries and expectations, which can prevent potential issues from arising in the future.

3. Listen carefully:

When dealing with difficult clients, it's important to listen carefully to their concerns and complaints. Often, clients may feel frustrated or upset because they don't feel heard or understood. By actively listening to their concerns, you can demonstrate that you are taking their feedback seriously and that you are committed to finding a solution that works for everyone.

To listen carefully, it's important to give the client your undivided attention. This means avoiding distractions like checking your phone or browsing the internet while you're talking to them. It also means paying attention to both their words and their tone of voice.

When the client is speaking, avoid interrupting them and try to clarify any points that you're unclear about. You can do this by asking open-ended questions like "Can you tell me more about that?" or "What specifically are you looking for?" This shows the client that you are engaged in the conversation and that you are working to understand their needs.

4. Be patient:

Being patient is an important skill when dealing with difficult clients. Sometimes, clients may not communicate their needs effectively or may have unrealistic expectations, which can lead to frustration and stress. It is important to remember that everyone has their own way of communicating and processing information, and it may take time to fully understand their needs and concerns. Rushing the process or reacting in an impatient manner can worsen the situation and make it more difficult to find a resolution.

In addition, being patient can help to build trust and rapport with the client. By taking the time to listen to their concerns, understand their perspective, and provide thoughtful responses, you can demonstrate your commitment to their project and show that you are invested in their success. This can help to establish a positive working relationship and may lead to additional opportunities in the future. Overall, while it can be challenging to remain patient in the face of difficult clients, it is an important skill that can benefit both you and the client in the long run.

5. Set clear boundaries:

Setting clear boundaries is an important aspect of managing difficult clients. It involves establishing and communicating clear expectations about what you can and cannot do, what the client can expect from you, and what the consequences will be if the client crosses those boundaries. The key is to be firm and consistent in enforcing those boundaries. Here are some tips for setting clear boundaries:

- Define your scope of work: Before starting any project, clearly define the scope of work and what it entails. This includes the deliverables, deadlines, and any limitations. Communicate this clearly to the client and get their agreement in writing. This will help to avoid any misunderstandings or disagreements later on.
- Be clear about communication channels and availability:

Establish how you will communicate with the client and how often. Let them know what hours you are available and how long they can expect to wait for a response. This will help to manage their expectations and avoid any frustration on either side. Make sure to stick to your communication plan and respond to their messages within a reasonable time frame.

6. Offer solutions:

When dealing with difficult clients, it's important to focus on finding solutions to the issues they are facing. Instead of simply pointing out problems or saying no to requests, try to come up with alternative solutions that meet the client's needs while also aligning with your own boundaries and abilities. This requires a combination of creativity, problem-solving skills, and a willingness to collaborate.

To offer effective solutions, it's important to first understand the client's underlying needs and goals. Ask questions to clarify their concerns and identify any constraints they may be facing. Then, brainstorm different options that address those concerns while also taking into account your own abilities and limitations. Be open to trying new approaches or adapting your usual way of working to better serve the client's needs. By offering proactive and creative solutions, you can show the client that you are invested in their success and committed to finding a mutually beneficial resolution.

7. Know when to walk away:

Knowing when to walk away from a difficult client is an important skill for freelancers. While it can be tempting to stick with a client even when things are not going well, it is important to recognize when a situation is not salvageable and it is time to move on. One of the key signs that it may be time to walk away is if the client is consistently disrespectful or unprofessional. If the client is belittling, insulting, or generally unpleasant to work with, it may be time to end the working relationship.

Another sign that it may be time to walk away is if the project scope or requirements have changed significantly without appropriate compensation or renegotiation. If a client is constantly adding on new requests or changing the project goals without offering additional payment, it may be time to reevaluate the working relationship. It is important to have clear boundaries and to be able to communicate your expectations and limitations to the client. If they are unable or unwilling to respect these boundaries, it may be time to walk away. Walking away from a difficult client can be difficult, but it is important to prioritize your own well-being and professional reputation.

8 .Stay in control :

Always make sure that you are in total control of the situation. The minute you let the client steer the conversation, you have lost it. This goes hand in hand with staying calm and collected. It helps you to steer the conversation in the direction you want, otherwise the client getting the upper hand will not be pretty.

Some clients can be manipulative, and once you let them dominate the situation, you might incur losses if they demand refunds, or replacement of products. Staying in control ensures you get to the root cause of the issue, and solve it before it gets out of hand.

9. Keep checking on them:

As much as you might not want to keep in contact with the difficult client, it is inevitable. You need to monitor how they are doing. Keep track of any transaction you might have with them by making sure it is going as planned.

When dealing with a difficult client, the slightest lapse in your plans may develop into a huge row that you can avoid by just being vigilant. Check with them on a regular basis, making sure everything is in place and the customer feels valued. This way, the customer has less to complain about, unless they are just being a nuisance.

10. Record everything:

If you are dealing with a client who keeps changing their mind at every turn, make sure you record every transaction and every conversation. It is incredibly frustrating having to deal with someone who keeps changing their mind, or insisting on something you clearly did not agree on.

11. Be careful what you say:

Sometimes it is more about what and how you say it. You have to be careful that your language does not display subtle aggression, which angers the client more. You may say something to a client that may sound normal to you, but it instead sounds condescending.

Listen to the kind of language your client uses, and try to counter that if they are the aggressive type. Choose your words with care. If your client uses aggressive words or insults, stay calm, no matter how much you want to bite the client's head off! Your choice of words will make the situation either worse or better.

Remember, dealing with difficult clients is a normal part of freelancing. With patience, professionalism, and effective communication, you can work through their issues and maintain a successful freelancing career.

MANAGING YOUR FINANCES

Setting rates and pricing your services:

When it comes to freelancing, setting rates and pricing your services can be a daunting task. However, it is essential to establish your value and ensure that your income is sustainable. Here are some tips for setting rates and pricing your services:

1. Research the market: Start by researching what other freelancers in your field are charging. This will give you an idea of the going rate and help you determine a competitive price for your services.

2. Determine your expenses: Before setting your rates, it's important to know your expenses. Calculate your costs, including overhead expenses such as software, hardware, and workspace. Also, factor in taxes, healthcare, and retirement savings.

3. Consider your experience and expertise: Your rates should reflect your experience and expertise. If you're just starting, your rates will likely be lower than someone with years of experience. However, as you gain experience and build your portfolio, you can adjust your rates accordingly.

4. Remember when you just starting on a particular platform without any previous feedback, you may need to start with a relatively low rate even if you have some experience because you need to have an advantage over the others. You can consider this as investing in yourself and after you get your first feedback you can raise your rate.

5. Determine your hourly rate or project rate: Decide whether you want to charge an hourly rate or a project rate. An hourly rate is ideal for projects with an uncertain scope or timeline. A project rate is a flat fee for a specific project, and it's perfect for well-defined

projects with a clear scope of work.

6. Be flexible: Be open to negotiating your rates with clients. Consider offering discounts for long-term projects or bulk orders. However, always ensure that your rates are sustainable and reflect the value of your services.

In conclusion, setting rates and pricing your services is an essential part of managing your finances as a freelancer. Do your research, consider your expenses, expertise, and experience, determine your hourly or project rate, and be flexible in negotiating with clients.

Managing Invoices and Payments

Managing invoices and payments is an essential part of freelancing. Here are some tips on how to manage your invoices and payments effectively:

1. Establish clear payment terms: Before starting any project, make sure to establish clear payment terms with the client. This includes the payment method, payment schedule, and any late payment fees or penalties.
2. Create professional invoices: Create professional invoices that include all the necessary information such as your name, business name, client name, payment due date, payment amount, and payment method. You can use software tools like FreshBooks, QuickBooks, or Wave to create professional invoices.
3. Send invoices on time: Send invoices promptly and ensure that you adhere to the payment schedule that was agreed upon with the client. Make sure to follow up with the client if payment is not received by the due date.
4. In case of Hourly jobs, you will probably use a platform built-in time tracker but some platforms don't have one, so you may need to use external tracker as Toggl. But any way it is a good practice to make a weekly time sheet to explain to the client how you spent the hours and the tasks details during these hours.
5. Keep track of all invoices and payments: It is important to keep track of all your invoices and payments. This can be done using a spreadsheet or an accounting software tool. This will help you to easily identify any outstanding payments and ensure that you receive payment for all completed work.
6. Follow up on late payments: If a payment is not received by the due date, follow up with the client to ensure

that they are aware of the outstanding payment. Be professional and polite when communicating with the client, but also assertive in ensuring that you receive payment for the work that you have completed.

7. Consider using payment platforms: Payment platforms like PayPal, Stripe, Payoneer and TransferWise can make it easier to receive payments from clients. These platforms offer features like recurring payments, payment reminders, and automatic transfers, which can simplify the payment process and help you get paid on time.

Tracking your expenses and file taxes

As a freelancer, it is important to keep track of your expenses and file taxes correctly in order to maintain financial stability and avoid any legal issues. Here are some tips for managing your finances and filing taxes:

1. Keep track of all your business expenses: This includes any expenses related to your work such as equipment, software, office space, internet bills, travel expenses, and more. Make sure to save receipts and invoices for each expense.

2. Separate personal and business finances: It's important to have separate bank accounts and credit cards for your personal and business finances. This helps you keep track of your business expenses and makes it easier to file taxes.

3. Use accounting software: There are several accounting software programs available, such as QuickBooks, that can help you manage your finances more efficiently. These tools can help you track your expenses, create invoices, and generate financial reports.

4. Hire a tax professional: Freelancers have unique tax requirements, so it's important to work with a tax professional who can help you navigate tax laws and ensure you file correctly. A tax professional can also help you identify deductions and minimize your tax liability.

5. Set aside money for taxes: As a freelancer, you're responsible for paying your own taxes. It's important to set aside a portion of your income each month for taxes so that you're prepared when tax season arrives.

6. File taxes on time: Make sure to file your taxes on time to avoid penalties and interest charges. The deadline for filing taxes in the US is typically April 15th, but this may vary depending on your country or region.

By following these tips, you can stay on top of your finances and avoid any issues when it comes to taxes and expenses.

BUILDING YOUR BRAND

Building your brand as a freelancer is about establishing a strong and consistent image for yourself in the minds of your clients and potential clients. This involves creating a unique identity that sets you apart from other freelancers and showcases your skills and expertise. To build your brand, you should focus on developing a strong online presence through your website and social media profiles, as well as creating high-quality content that showcases your skills and expertise. You should also focus on networking and building relationships with clients and other freelancers in your industry, as well as seeking out opportunities to showcase your work and expertise through speaking engagements and other events. By building a strong brand, you can establish yourself as a trusted and reputable freelancer and attract more clients and opportunities to grow your business.

Creating a personal brand that aligns with your niche.

Creating a personal brand is an important aspect of building your freelancing business. Your personal brand should reflect your niche and the services you offer, as well as your unique strengths and values. To start building your brand, you should first identify your niche and the type of clients you want to attract. This will help you create a brand message that speaks directly to your target audience.

Once you have identified your niche, you should create a brand identity that reflects your unique style and personality. This can include a logo, color scheme, and typography that are consistent across all of your marketing materials, including your website, business cards, and social media profiles.

It's also important to create content that showcases your expertise and demonstrates your value to potential clients. This can include blog posts, case studies, and other types of content that provide insight into your industry and the services you offer. By consistently creating high-quality content, you can establish yourself as a thought leader in your niche and build trust with potential clients.

Finally, it's important to promote your personal brand through various marketing channels, such as social media, email marketing, and networking events. By building a strong personal brand, you can differentiate yourself from competitors and establish a reputation as a skilled and trustworthy freelancer.

Developing a strong online presence

Developing a strong online presence is crucial for any freelancer who wants to build their brand and attract clients. Here are some key steps to help you develop a strong online presence:

1. Create a professional website: A professional website is your online storefront and the foundation of your online presence. It should showcase your work, services, and contact information in a clear and concise manner.

2. Establish a social media presence: Choose social media platforms that align with your target audience and niche, and create a strong and consistent brand across all platforms. Regularly post relevant content and engage with your followers to increase your visibility and credibility.

3. Build a portfolio: A portfolio showcases your best work and demonstrates your skills and experience. It should be easy to navigate and highlight your unique value proposition.

4. Get listed on freelance platforms: Joining established freelance platforms like Upwork, Freelancer.com, or Fiverr can help you get discovered by clients who are actively seeking freelancers in your niche.

5. Network and collaborate: Building relationships with other freelancers, industry experts, and potential clients can help you expand your reach and gain valuable insights and referrals.

By implementing these strategies, you can establish a strong online presence that will help you stand out from the competition and attract more clients.

AHMED ATA

Creating a marketing strategy to promote your services

Creating a marketing strategy is important to promote your services and attract potential clients. Here are some steps to develop a strong marketing strategy:

1. Identify your target audience: Before creating a marketing strategy, you need to identify your target audience. Who are they? What are their needs and pain points? How can you help solve their problems with your services?

2. Create a unique value proposition: You need to have a unique value proposition that differentiates you from your competitors. It should clearly communicate the benefits of your services to your target audience.

3. Choose your marketing channels: Based on your target audience and unique value proposition, you need to choose the most effective marketing channels to reach them. This can include social media platforms, email marketing, content marketing, paid advertising, etc.

4. Develop a content strategy: Content marketing is an effective way to showcase your expertise and build your brand. You can create blog posts, videos, social media content, case studies, and other types of content that demonstrate your skills and value.

5. Engage with your audience: It's important to engage with your audience on social media and other platforms. Respond to comments and messages, participate in relevant groups and communities, and provide helpful information and insights.

6. Measure and adjust: Finally, you need to measure the effectiveness of your marketing strategy and make adjustments as needed. Use analytics tools to track your website traffic, social media engagement, and other

metrics to see what's working and what's not. Then, adjust your strategy accordingly to maximize your results.

MANAGING YOUR TIME AND PRODUCTIVITY

Managing your time and productivity as a freelancer is crucial for your success. It involves setting clear goals, prioritizing tasks, creating a schedule, and eliminating distractions. By effectively managing your time, you can increase your productivity, meet deadlines, and maintain a healthy work-life balance. It also helps you stay focused and organized, allowing you to deliver high-quality work to your clients efficiently.

Setting up a schedule and sticking to it

Setting up a schedule and sticking to it is essential for managing your time and maximizing your productivity as a freelancer. Here are some steps to help you establish and maintain a productive schedule:

1. Identify your most productive hours: Determine the times of day when you feel most focused and energized. This can vary from person to person, so identify the hours when you can do your best work.
2. Prioritize your tasks: Make a list of all the tasks you need to accomplish and prioritize them based on importance and deadlines. This helps you allocate your time effectively and ensure that you complete critical tasks first.
3. Allocate time blocks: Divide your day into specific time blocks dedicated to different types of tasks. For example, you can have separate blocks for client work, marketing, administrative tasks, and personal breaks. This helps you focus on specific activities during each block and avoid multitasking.
4. Use productivity tools: Utilize digital tools or apps such as calendars, task management apps as to-do programs as Trello, or project management tools as Jira to organize and schedule your tasks. Set reminders and deadlines to stay on track.
5. Be realistic with your time estimates: Estimate how much time each task will take and allocate sufficient time for each. Be realistic and consider factors like research, revisions, and unexpected challenges. Leave buffer time between tasks to account for unforeseen circumstances.
6. Minimize distractions: Identify and minimize

distractions that can hinder your productivity, such as social media, email notifications, or noisy environments. Consider using productivity techniques like the Pomodoro Technique, where you work for a focused period and take short breaks in between.

7. Monitor and adjust: Regularly evaluate how well you stick to your schedule and identify areas for improvement. Keep track of how much time you spend on each task and adjust your schedule accordingly to optimize your productivity.

Remember that while it's important to follow your schedule, be flexible enough to accommodate unexpected changes or urgent tasks that may arise. By setting up a schedule and committing to it, you can effectively manage your time, increase your productivity, and achieve your goals as a freelancer.

Delegating tasks and outsourcing

Delegating tasks and outsourcing is an important aspect of managing your workload and optimizing your productivity as a freelancer. Here's a detailed guide on how to effectively delegate tasks and outsource:

1. Assess your strengths and weaknesses: Identify the tasks or areas where you excel and those where you may need assistance or lack expertise. This helps you determine which tasks are suitable for delegation or outsourcing.

2. Define the scope of work: Clearly define the tasks or projects you want to delegate or outsource. Break them down into specific deliverables and set clear expectations in terms of quality, deadlines, and any other requirements.

3. Identify suitable candidates or service providers: Seek out freelancers, professionals, or agencies who specialize in the tasks you want to delegate or outsource. Look for individuals or companies with relevant experience, positive reviews or recommendations, and a track record of delivering high-quality work.

4. Communicate effectively: Clearly communicate your expectations, requirements, and any necessary guidelines or instructions to the individuals or companies you're delegating or outsourcing to. Provide all the relevant project details, access to necessary resources, and establish a clear channel for ongoing communication.

5. Set milestones and checkpoints: Break the delegated or outsourced tasks into manageable milestones or checkpoints. This allows you to track progress, provide feedback, and make any necessary adjustments along the way.

6. Maintain regular communication: Keep an open line of communication with the individuals or companies you've delegated or outsourced to. Regularly check in on progress, address any concerns or questions, and ensure that the work is proceeding according to plan.

7. Provide feedback and guidance: Offer constructive feedback and guidance to the individuals or companies you're working with. This helps them understand your expectations better and make any necessary improvements.

8. Monitor and review performance: Regularly assess the performance of the delegated or outsourced tasks. Evaluate the quality of work, adherence to deadlines, and overall effectiveness. If needed, provide additional guidance or make adjustments to ensure the desired outcomes are achieved.

9. Maintain confidentiality and security: If you're delegating or outsourcing tasks that involve sensitive information or intellectual property, ensure that proper confidentiality agreements are in place. Protect your data and assets by working with trustworthy individuals or companies.

10. Evaluate cost-effectiveness: Consider the financial aspect of delegation and outsourcing. Assess the cost-benefit ratio and determine if it's more cost-effective to delegate or outsource certain tasks rather than handling them yourself. Factor in the quality of work, time saved, and the potential for greater efficiency or revenue generation.

By effectively delegating tasks and outsourcing, you can focus on your core strengths, manage your workload more efficiently, and leverage the expertise of others to deliver high-quality results to your clients. It allows you to scale your business, take on more projects, and maintain a healthy work-life balance.

Cooperate With Other Freelancers To Take On More Complex Jobs

Forming groups or agencies with other freelancers can be a strategic approach to take on more complex jobs and offer a broader range of services. Here's a detailed guide on how to form such groups:

1. Identify complementary skills: Look for freelancers who possess skills that complement yours and align with the services you want to offer as a group. For example, if you're a web developer, you may want to collaborate with a designer, a copywriter, and a digital marketer to provide comprehensive website solutions.
2. Establish clear roles and responsibilities: Clearly define the roles and responsibilities of each member within the group or agency. This ensures that everyone knows their tasks, avoids overlaps or gaps in work, and maintains efficient collaboration.
3. Create a shared vision and goals: Discuss and align on the group's vision, mission, and long-term goals. This shared understanding will guide decision-making and keep everyone motivated and focused.
4. Define communication and workflow processes: Establish effective communication channels and protocols for sharing information, discussing projects, and managing tasks. Determine how you'll collaborate, share files, and provide feedback to ensure smooth workflow and timely delivery.
5. Create a legal structure: Consider formalizing your group or agency by creating a legal structure, such as a partnership or limited liability company (LLC). Consult with legal professionals to determine the most suitable structure for your situation and to address any

contractual agreements or liabilities.

6. Develop a shared portfolio and brand identity: Create a portfolio that showcases the collective work of the group or agency. This demonstrates your combined expertise and gives potential clients a clear understanding of the services you offer. Establish a consistent brand identity that represents your collective values and style.

7. Collaborate on marketing and business development: Work together to market your services, reach out to potential clients, and secure projects. Pool your resources and networks to expand your reach and increase the chances of attracting larger, more complex jobs.

8. Maintain open and transparent communication: Foster a culture of open communication and transparency within the group or agency. Regularly hold meetings or check-ins to discuss progress, address concerns, and make any necessary adjustments to enhance collaboration and client satisfaction.

9. Establish a fair compensation structure: Determine how you'll split revenues and allocate profits among group members. Consider factors such as the level of contribution, expertise, and the complexity of individual roles to ensure a fair compensation structure.

10. Continuously evaluate and adapt: Regularly assess the group's performance, review client feedback, and identify areas for improvement. Adapt your processes, workflows, or team composition as needed to optimize efficiency, quality, and client satisfaction.

By forming groups or agencies with other freelancers, you can leverage collective skills and resources to take on more complex projects, expand your service offerings, and increase your overall competitiveness in the market.

AHMED ATA

Avoiding burnout and stay motivated

Avoiding burnout is essential for maintaining your productivity and overall well-being as a freelancer. Here's a detailed guide on how to prevent burnout and stay motivated:

1. Prioritize self-care: Make self-care a priority by taking care of your physical, mental, and emotional well-being. Get enough sleep, eat nutritious meals, engage in regular exercise, and take breaks throughout the day to recharge.

2. Set realistic goals: Set achievable goals that align with your capabilities and workload. Break down larger projects into smaller, manageable tasks to avoid feeling overwhelmed. Celebrate your accomplishments along the way to stay motivated.

3. Establish work-life boundaries: Define clear boundaries between your work and personal life. Set specific working hours and avoid overworking. Disconnect from work during non-working hours to recharge and engage in activities that bring you joy.

4. Practice time management: Effectively manage your time by prioritizing tasks, creating schedules, and setting deadlines. Avoid procrastination and stay organized to reduce stress and increase productivity.

5. Vary your work routine: Incorporate variety into your work routine to keep things interesting and prevent monotony. Alternate between different projects or tasks, try new approaches or techniques, and explore creative outlets to stay motivated.

6. Seek support and connection: Engage with other freelancers or professionals in your field for support, networking, and collaboration opportunities. Join online communities or attend industry events

to connect with like-minded individuals and share experiences.

7. Find inspiration and motivation: Surround yourself with sources of inspiration and motivation. Follow industry influencers, read books or articles related to your field, and seek out opportunities for continuous learning and skill development.
8. Take regular breaks and vacations: Allow yourself to take regular breaks throughout the day to rest and recharge. Additionally, plan and take vacations or time off to fully disconnect from work and rejuvenate.
9. Manage stress effectively: Implement stress management techniques such as mindfulness, meditation, deep breathing exercises, or engaging in hobbies or activities that help you relax. Find what works best for you to manage stress and incorporate it into your routine.
10. Reflect and reassess: Regularly reflect on your work, accomplishments, and overall satisfaction. Assess whether you're still aligned with your professional goals and make necessary adjustments or changes to maintain motivation and avoid burnout.

Remember, it's important to listen to your body and mind. If you start feeling overwhelmed, fatigued, or excessively stressed, take a step back and reassess your workload and self-care practices. Prioritizing your well-being will ultimately contribute to your long-term success and enjoyment as a freelancer.

EXPANING YOUR FREELANCING BUSINESS

Planning for the future of your freelance career

Planning for the future of your freelance career involves setting goals, evaluating your progress, and making strategic decisions to ensure long-term success. Here's a detailed explanation of how to plan for the future of your freelance career:

1. Define your long-term goals: Clearly define your long-term goals for your freelance career. These could include financial targets, professional achievements, personal development, or work-life balance. Having a clear vision of what you want to achieve will guide your decision-making and help you stay focused.

2. Assess your current situation: Evaluate your current freelance business, including your client base, income, skills, and market trends. Identify your strengths, weaknesses, opportunities, and threats. This assessment will help you understand where you stand and identify areas for improvement or potential growth.

3. Identify your niche and target market: Determine your niche or specialized area of expertise within your industry. Understand the needs and preferences of your target market. This will allow you to position yourself effectively, differentiate from competitors, and attract the right clients.

4. Continuously learn and upskill: Invest in your professional development by staying updated with industry trends, technologies, and best practices. Identify areas where you can enhance your skills and knowledge. This will enable you to provide more value to clients, expand your service offerings, and stay competitive.

5. Diversify your income sources: Consider diversifying your income streams by exploring new services,

products, or markets. This can help you mitigate risk and create additional revenue streams. For example, you could offer consulting services, create digital products, or explore new industries or client segments.

6. Build a strong network: Cultivate relationships with fellow freelancers, industry professionals, and potential clients. Attend networking events, join online communities, and actively engage in conversations. Building a strong network can lead to collaboration opportunities, referrals, and valuable insights for your freelance career.

7. Plan for financial stability: Create a financial plan that includes budgeting, saving, and investing. Set aside funds for emergencies and unforeseen circumstances. Consider retirement planning and seek advice from financial professionals if needed. Having financial stability will provide a solid foundation for your freelance career and give you peace of mind.

8. Adapt to industry changes: Stay adaptable and flexible in response to evolving market trends, technology advancements, and client demands. Embrace new tools, platforms, or methodologies that can enhance your work efficiency and effectiveness. Be willing to adapt your skills and services to meet the changing needs of your clients.

9. Evaluate and adjust your plans regularly: Regularly review and evaluate your progress towards your goals. Assess the effectiveness of your strategies and make necessary adjustments. Stay agile and open to pivoting if needed to align with market demands or personal aspirations.

By planning for the future of your freelance career, you can position yourself for continued growth, fulfillment, and long-term success. Remember that planning is an ongoing process, and it's important to regularly reassess and adapt your plans to stay relevant and achieve your desired outcomes.

DEALING WITH CHANLLENGES

Handling difficult clients

Business is not, and has never been, for the faint-hearted. Some clients may cause you enough grief to make you want to drop them, or worse, quit the business

To know how to deal with difficult clients we should first know what are the types of clients and their personalities. Freelancers can encounter a variety of client personalities while working on different projects. Here are some common types of clients by personality that a freelancer may come across:

1. The Ideal Client: This type of client is a dream to work with. They clearly communicate their requirements, provide constructive feedback, and respect your expertise. They appreciate your work and value your contributions, making the collaboration smooth and enjoyable.

2. The Micromanager: This client wants to be involved in every step of the project and may have a tendency to micromanage. They may provide excessive instructions, require frequent updates, and request multiple revisions. While challenging, it's important to maintain open communication and set clear expectations to establish boundaries and ensure a successful outcome.

3. The Indecisive Client: This client struggles with decision-making and may change their requirements or direction frequently. They may be unsure about their vision or have difficulty providing specific feedback. As a freelancer, it's important to be patient, offer guidance, and establish clear processes to help them make decisions effectively.

4. The Demanding Client: This client has high expectations and may be demanding in terms of quality, timelines, or scope. They may push for tight deadlines or request additional work without adjusting the

budget. Freelancers dealing with demanding clients should clearly communicate their capabilities, manage expectations, and set boundaries to maintain a healthy working relationship.

5. The Collaborative Client: This client values collaboration and seeks input from freelancers as part of the creative process. They appreciate your expertise and actively involve you in discussions, brainstorming, and decision-making. Collaborative clients provide an opportunity to showcase your skills and contribute to the project's success.

6. The Difficult Client: This type of client may exhibit challenging behaviors such as being rude, disrespectful, or unresponsive. They may have unrealistic expectations or be overly critical. Freelancers should remain professional, communicate assertively, and try to address concerns or issues through open dialogue. In some cases, it may be necessary to reassess the working relationship if the difficulties persist.

7. The Value-Driven Client: This client focuses on the value and outcomes they expect from the project rather than solely on the cost. They appreciate the expertise and quality you bring to the table and are willing to invest accordingly. Freelancers should highlight the value they can deliver and align their services with the client's desired outcomes.

8. Clients who don't know what they want: These clients may have a vague idea of what they need but struggle to articulate their requirements clearly. As a freelancer, it's important to ask probing questions, provide guidance, and offer suggestions to help them define their goals and project scope.

9. Clients who underestimate your work: Some clients may not fully appreciate the value or complexity of the work

you provide. They may expect quick and cheap solutions without understanding the time, effort, and expertise required. Freelancers should educate these clients about the value they bring and demonstrate the benefits of investing in quality work.

10. Clients who ask you to reduce your price at the last minute: These clients may try to negotiate or bargain for a lower price after the project details have been agreed upon. As a freelancer, it's important to stick to your pricing structure and communicate the value you offer. If necessary, you can explain the reasons for your rates and the scope of the project, but be cautious about undervaluing your services.

11. Clients who nitpick: Some clients may have a tendency to excessively scrutinize or find faults in your work. They may request numerous revisions or make unnecessary changes. It's essential to set clear expectations from the beginning, establish revision limits, and ensure open communication to address their concerns while maintaining the project's progress.

12. Clients who disappear: These clients may suddenly become unresponsive or stop communicating during the project. They may not provide timely feedback or clarification, causing delays and uncertainty. Freelancers should maintain regular communication, set clear deadlines, and establish a protocol for handling unresponsive clients to mitigate the impact on the project timeline.

13. Clients who are always on: These clients may expect immediate responses and have high demands for your availability. They may contact you outside of agreed-upon working hours or require constant updates. It's important to establish clear boundaries, communicate your availability and response times, and manage their expectations regarding communication and availability.

14. Clients who don't want to pay: Unfortunately, some clients may try to avoid paying or delay payments. It's crucial to have a clear payment policy and contract in place before starting the project. Clearly outline payment terms, milestones, and consequences for non-payment. If issues arise, communicate assertively and be prepared to escalate the matter if necessary.

You can cope with even your most difficult client in several ways, which will leave both you and the client satisfied.

1. Be detail specific: Pay close attention to the details of the project and client requirements. Ensure you have a thorough understanding of their expectations and deliverables. Being detail-specific allows you to provide accurate solutions, demonstrate your professionalism, and minimize misunderstandings.
2. Keep checking on them: Maintain regular communication with the client to keep them updated on the progress of the project. Regular check-ins show your dedication and commitment to the project. It also provides an opportunity to address any concerns or issues promptly, avoiding potential conflicts.
3. Empathize even if you don't agree: Put yourself in the client's shoes and try to understand their perspective. Even if you don't agree with their point of view, empathizing demonstrates your willingness to listen and find common ground. It can help diffuse tense situations and foster better communication.
4. Record everything: Keep a record of all communications, agreements, and changes throughout the project. This includes emails, conversations, and any modifications to the scope or timeline. Documentation serves as evidence in case of disputes or misunderstandings, ensuring clarity and accountability.

5. Be an active listener: Practice active listening by giving your full attention to the client's concerns or feedback. Avoid interrupting and genuinely try to understand their needs. Reflecting back their thoughts or summarizing their points shows that you value their input and are actively engaged in finding solutions.
6. Be careful what you say: Choose your words thoughtfully and avoid responding in a defensive or confrontational manner, even if the client becomes difficult or challenging. Maintain a professional and respectful tone in all your communications. Diplomacy and tact can help de-escalate conflicts and maintain a positive working relationship.
7. Learn to tell when it's a difference in personalities: Recognize that conflicts may arise due to differences in personalities or working styles. It's important to remain objective and not take it personally. Focus on finding common ground and understanding the client's preferences to adapt your approach accordingly.
8. Set goals: Establish clear goals and objectives for the project in collaboration with the client. Clearly define the deliverables, milestones, and timelines. Setting goals provides a shared understanding of expectations and helps manage client expectations throughout the project.
9. Learn how to let go: In some cases, despite your best efforts, a client may not be satisfied or may be excessively demanding. It's important to recognize when the working relationship becomes detrimental to your well-being or productivity. Sometimes, it's better to part ways amicably and focus on clients who appreciate your work and professionalism.
10. Stay in control: Maintain control over the situation by staying calm, professional, and assertive. Avoid

getting drawn into arguments or letting difficult clients disrupt your workflow. Take proactive steps to address issues, set boundaries, and manage expectations. Your professionalism and confidence can influence how the client perceives and interacts with you.

By following these tips, you can navigate challenging situations with difficult clients more effectively. It helps maintain professionalism, promotes better communication, and enhances the overall client-freelancer relationship.

Managing project scope and deadlines

Managing project scope and deadlines is a critical aspect of freelancing that ensures successful project delivery and client satisfaction. It involves effectively defining the scope of work, setting clear objectives, and establishing realistic timelines to accomplish the project goals. Here are some key considerations for managing project scope and deadlines:

1. Scope Definition: Begin by clearly understanding the project requirements and discussing them with the client. Define the scope of work, including deliverables, tasks, and any limitations or exclusions. Document the agreed-upon scope in a project proposal or contract to avoid scope creep.

2. Task Breakdown: Break down the project into manageable tasks and subtasks. Assign estimated durations and dependencies to each task. This helps in creating a comprehensive project plan and timeline.

3. Establish Realistic Deadlines: Set realistic deadlines for each task based on the scope, complexity, and available resources. Consider factors like your own workload, client availability for feedback, and potential external dependencies.

4. Prioritize and Sequencing: Prioritize tasks based on their criticality and impact on project success. Determine the logical sequencing of tasks, ensuring that dependencies are addressed and that work progresses smoothly.

5. Communication and Expectation Management:

Regularly communicate with the client to manage expectations and keep them informed about project progress. Provide updates on milestones, any potential delays, and any necessary scope adjustments. This helps in maintaining transparency and managing client satisfaction.

6. Proactive Risk Management: Identify potential risks and challenges that could impact project scope or deadlines. Create contingency plans to mitigate these risks and address any issues promptly to minimize their impact on the project schedule.

7. Time Tracking and Monitoring: Implement a system to track your time spent on each task and monitor progress against the project plan. This helps in identifying any deviations from the schedule early on, allowing for timely adjustments and corrective actions.

8. Flexibility and Adaptability: Recognize that project scope and deadlines may need to be adjusted due to unforeseen circumstances or client requests. Stay flexible and adaptable while ensuring that any scope changes are properly documented, communicated, and agreed upon with the client.

By effectively managing project scope and deadlines, you can ensure that projects are completed within the defined parameters, maintain client satisfaction, and build a reputation for delivering quality work on time.

Coping with periods of low income

Coping with periods of low income can be a challenging aspect of freelancing. However, with proper planning and strategies, it's possible to navigate these situations effectively. Here's an explanation of how to cope with periods of low income:

1. Budget and financial planning: Create a realistic budget that reflects your current financial situation and consider your essential expenses. Evaluate your spending habits and identify areas where you can cut back or save money. Prioritize necessary expenses while minimizing discretionary spending. By having a clear understanding of your financial obligations and resources, you can better manage your finances during periods of low income.

2. Emergency fund: Establish an emergency fund to provide a financial cushion during lean times. Save a portion of your income when business is good, and set it aside for emergencies or low-income periods. Having a reserve of funds can help alleviate stress and provide a safety net when you experience fluctuations in income.

3. Diversify your income streams: Explore opportunities to diversify your income by offering additional services or exploring alternative sources of revenue. This can involve expanding your client base, seeking project-based work, or exploring passive income streams such as online courses or affiliate marketing. Diversification can help mitigate the impact of a slowdown in one area of your freelance business.

4. Creating profiles on multiple freelancing platforms allows you to diversify your client base and expand your reach. Each platform attracts different clients and offers unique opportunities, so by being present on multiple platforms, you increase your chances of securing

projects even when business is slow on one platform.

5. Seek short-term or part-time work: Consider taking up short-term or part-time work to supplement your income during low periods. This could involve freelance gigs, consulting projects, or even traditional employment. Look for opportunities that align with your skills and schedule, allowing you to bridge the income gap until your freelance business picks up again.

6. Upskill and invest in professional development: Use periods of low income to invest in yourself and enhance your skills. Seek out training programs, courses, or certifications that can expand your expertise and make you more marketable. Increasing your skillset can open up new opportunities and potentially lead to higher-paying projects in the future.

7. Network and market yourself: Stay active in your professional network and maintain connections with clients, colleagues, and industry contacts. Inform them of your availability and expertise, and leverage word-of-mouth referrals to secure new projects. Utilize online platforms, social media, and professional networking events to market your services and attract potential clients.

8. Negotiate payment terms: When entering into new contracts or projects, consider negotiating favorable payment terms that provide some stability during low-income periods. For example, you could request partial upfront payments or milestone-based payments to ensure a steady cash flow. Clear payment agreements and invoices can help minimize payment delays and ensure you receive timely compensation for your work.

9. Stay motivated and positive: It's crucial to maintain a positive mindset during periods of low income. Focus on the long-term goals of your freelance career and remind

yourself that low-income periods are temporary. Use the downtime to reevaluate and improve your business strategies, enhance your skills, and explore new opportunities. Maintaining motivation and a proactive approach can help you bounce back stronger.

By implementing these strategies, you can better cope with periods of low income as a freelancer. It's important to remember that freelancing often involves fluctuations in income, and planning ahead and taking proactive measures can help you navigate these challenges more effectively.

CONCLUSION AND NEXT STEPS

Reflecting on your freelance journey

Embarking on a freelance journey is like stepping onto a winding path full of exhilarating highs and unexpected twists. As you navigate through the realm of self-employment, you encounter a myriad of experiences, challenges, and triumphs that shape your professional growth. Amidst the constant hustle and the ever-changing landscape, it is crucial to pause and reflect on your freelance journey. Reflecting allows you to unravel the hidden gems of wisdom buried within your experiences and offers a compass to guide you towards future success. So, take a moment to walk down memory lane, celebrate your victories, learn from your missteps, and envision the path ahead. In this section, we delve into the art of reflecting on your freelance journey, uncovering its transformative power to shape your skills, mindset, and aspirations. Let's explore the profound insights and invaluable lessons that lie in the depths of self-reflection as you embark on this introspective adventure of personal and professional growth.

Here's an explanation of the importance and process of reflecting on your freelance journey:

1. Gain self-awareness: Reflection allows you to gain a deeper understanding of yourself as a freelancer. It helps you identify your strengths, weaknesses, and areas for improvement. By reflecting on your past projects, successes, and challenges, you can assess your skills, preferences, and working style. This self-awareness enables you to make informed decisions and align your freelance career with your values and goals.

2. Celebrate achievements: Reflecting on your freelance journey allows you to acknowledge and celebrate your achievements. It's an opportunity to recognize the milestones you've reached, the projects you've successfully completed, and the positive feedback or

testimonials you've received. Celebrating your successes boosts your confidence and motivation, reminding you of your capabilities and the progress you've made.

3. Learn from mistakes: Reflection helps you learn from your mistakes and setbacks. By analyzing projects that didn't go as planned or encounters with difficult clients, you can identify the factors that contributed to the challenges and find ways to prevent or address similar issues in the future. Learning from mistakes is essential for growth and professional development as a freelancer.

4. Identify areas for improvement: Through reflection, you can identify areas for improvement and skill development. It might involve recognizing gaps in your expertise, exploring new tools or technologies, or honing your communication or time management skills. By pinpointing these areas, you can proactively seek opportunities for learning and growth to enhance your capabilities as a freelancer.

5. Set future goals: Reflecting on your freelance journey helps you set meaningful and realistic goals for the future. It allows you to assess where you want to go, what you want to achieve, and the steps you need to take to get there. By understanding your strengths, weaknesses, and aspirations, you can set specific, measurable, achievable, relevant, and time-bound (SMART) goals that align with your vision for your freelance career.

To reflect on your freelance journey, set aside dedicated time to review your past projects, client interactions, and overall progress. Consider keeping a journal or document where you can record your reflections, insights, and lessons learned. Ask yourself questions such as: What have been my biggest accomplishments? What were the challenges I faced, and how did I overcome them? What skills or knowledge do I need to enhance? What are my future aspirations and goals? By engaging in this reflective process, you can gain valuable insights that inform your future decisions and actions as a freelancer.

Setting goals for the future

Imagine standing on the precipice of possibility, with a world of opportunities beckoning you forward. Setting goals for the future is like casting a vibrant tapestry of aspirations and dreams, weaving a roadmap that guides you towards your desired destination. It's a chance to channel your energy, focus your efforts, and unleash the full force of your potential. Whether you envision climbing towering peaks of success or charting unexplored territories of innovation, goal setting empowers you to carve a unique path in your freelance journey. With each goal you set, you ignite a spark of ambition that fuels your drive, propels you forward, and transforms dreams into tangible realities. So, take a leap into the realm of possibilities, where aspirations take flight, where dreams evolve into concrete targets, and where your future as a freelancer becomes a captivating adventure awaiting its grand unveiling. In this section, we embark on a quest to unravel the art of setting goals for the future, exploring the transformative power it holds to shape your trajectory, inspire your actions, and redefine the very essence of your freelance career. Let us embark on this thrilling expedition together, where the boundaries of imagination are boundless, and the tapestry of your future awaits its vibrant brushstrokes of achievement.

Next steps for growing and improving your freelance business

Congratulations! You've laid a solid foundation for your freelance business, but the journey doesn't end here. It's time to embark on the exhilarating quest of growing and improving your freelance empire, reaching new heights of success and fulfillment. As you set your sights on the horizon of possibilities, a world of opportunities awaits your eager embrace. The next steps will test your mettle, challenge your ingenuity, and fuel your insatiable hunger for growth. Get ready to unleash your creative prowess, expand your network, and harness the power of innovation.

First, expand your professional network like a weaver connecting threads in a grand tapestry. Attend industry events, join online communities, and engage in networking activities that expose you to like-minded professionals and potential clients. Cultivate genuine connections, collaborate with fellow freelancers, and seize opportunities for partnership and mutual growth. Remember, your network is not just a web of acquaintances; it's a vibrant ecosystem of support, mentorship, and collaboration.

Second, continuously sharpen your skills and evolve like a phoenix rising from the ashes. Stay abreast of industry trends, emerging technologies, and new methodologies relevant to your niche. Seek out training programs, online courses, and workshops that enhance your expertise and broaden your skill set. Embrace the thrill of learning and adaptability, for they are the keys that unlock doors to novel ventures and high-value projects.

Next, refine your brand identity with the finesse of a master artist adding delicate brushstrokes to a masterpiece. Craft a compelling personal brand that captures your unique essence and resonates with your target audience. Develop a captivating online presence through a well-designed website, engaging content, and a strong social media presence. Consistently showcase your expertise, share valuable insights, and build trust among potential clients who are drawn to your brand's authenticity and expertise.

Furthermore, embrace innovation and explore new avenues to diversify your income streams. Leverage your expertise to create digital products, launch online courses, or develop passive income streams such as e-books, templates, or software solutions. Think beyond the confines of traditional freelancing and let your entrepreneurial spirit soar as you unlock new sources of revenue and expand your impact in the marketplace.

Lastly, never underestimate the power of continuous improvement. Regularly assess your business processes, solicit feedback from clients, and reflect on your performance. Identify areas for refinement and implement strategies to enhance your efficiency, effectiveness, and client satisfaction. Embrace a growth mindset that thrives on constant evolution and adaptation.

So, my fellow freelancer, fasten your seatbelt, embrace the winds of change, and embark on this exhilarating journey of growth and improvement. Let your entrepreneurial spirit guide you, your passion ignite you, and your commitment drive you to new heights. The road may be challenging, but the rewards are immeasurable. It's time to embrace the next chapter of your freelance odyssey and revel in the thrill of building a thriving business that showcases your talent, fuels your passion, and leaves an indelible mark on the world.

THE END OF THE BOOK – THE START OF YOUR JOURNEY

As we reach the end of this freelancing book, I hope you've embarked on a transformative journey that has empowered you with knowledge, inspiration, and the tools to thrive in the world of freelancing. You've delved into the intricacies of freelancing, uncovering its boundless opportunities, navigating its challenges, and honing the skills and mindset necessary for success.

Remember, freelancing is not just a career choice; it's a way of life. It offers freedom, flexibility, and the chance to sculpt your own professional destiny. Embrace the entrepreneurial spirit within you, fuel your creativity, and continue to refine your craft with unwavering passion and dedication.

As you move forward, keep exploring new horizons, seizing opportunities, and adapting to the ever-evolving landscape of the freelance market. Embrace the power of self-reflection, goal-setting, and continuous improvement to stay ahead of the curve and achieve new heights of excellence.

But above all, cherish the connections you've made, the collaborations you've fostered, and the communities you've become a part of. Embrace the support of fellow freelancers, mentors, and clients who have believed in your talent and journeyed alongside you.

Freelancing is an adventure that never truly ends. It's an ever-unfolding story of growth, resilience, and self-discovery. So, my fellow freelancer, step into the future with confidence, purpose, and unwavering belief in your abilities. Embrace the unknown, celebrate your successes, learn from your failures, and let your freelance career become an extraordinary testament to the power of pursuing your passions.

Thank you for joining me on this incredible journey. May your freelancing path be filled with fulfillment, abundance, and endless possibilities. Here's to the next chapter of your extraordinary freelance odyssey!

References:

1. Anderson, M. (2018). The Freelancer's Bible: Everything You Need to Know to Have the Career of Your Dreams - On Your Terms. Workman Publishing Company.
2. Horowitz, L. (2019). Freelance: A Guide to Kickstarting Your Freelance Career. Freelance Creative Publishing.
3. Fish, M. (2019). The Ultimate Freelancer's Guidebook: Learn How to Land the Best Jobs, Build Your Brand, and Be Your Own Boss. Skyhorse Publishing.
4. Kim, B. (2018). The Gig Economy: The Complete Guide to Getting Better Work, Taking More Time Off, and Financing the Life You Want. AMACOM.
5. Perkins, R. (2017). Work for Yourself: A Guide to Success for People Who Work Outside the 9 to 5 Cube. Sourcebooks.
6. Vanderkam, L. (2016). Juliet's School of Possibilities: A Little Story About the Power of Priorities. Portfolio.
7. Pink, D. H. (2018). When: The Scientific Secrets of Perfect Timing. Riverhead Books.
8. Gerber, M. E. (2009). The E-Myth Revisited: Why Most Small Businesses Don't Work and What to Do About It. HarperBusiness.
9. Covey, S. R. (2004). The 7 Habits of Highly Effective People: Powerful Lessons in Personal Change. Free Press.
10. Newport, C. (2016). Deep Work: Rules for Focused Success in a Distracted World. Grand Central Publishing.

www.ingramcontent.com/pod-product-compliance
Lightning Source LLC
Chambersburg PA
CBHW070107230526
45472CB00004B/1158